Wat Your F*cking Language

NOTEBOOK

With A German, French, Spanish, Italian, Chinese, Japanese, Arabic Or Hindi Swear Word On Every Page

This Notebook Belongs To:

E-mail:

Phone:

GOALS:

- [ ]
- [ ]
- [ ]
- [ ]
- [ ]
- [ ]
- [ ]
- [ ]
- [ ]
- [ ]

Accomplishments:

- ○ _____
- ○ _____
- ○ _____
- ○ _____
- ○ _____
- ○ _____
- ○ _____
- ○ _____
- ○ _____
- ○ _____

Habit Tracker	1	2	3	4	5	6	7	8	9	10

Appointments & Special Dates:

In German, 'Schnoodle Noodle' means: Dick Snot

In Spanish, 'Verga' means: Fucking Bastard

In French, 'Le Con, La Chatte' means: Cunt, Pussy

In Spanish, 'Payaso' means: Fucking Bastard

In French, 'Lèche Mon Cul ' means: Kiss My Ass

In Japanese, 'Onani' means: Masterbate

In Arabic, 'Khara Beek' means: Shit In You (Male)

In French, 'Tapette, Pedale' means: You Faggot Fuck

In Japanese, 'Roba' means: Donkey

In Arabic, 'Zib' means: Penis

In Arabic, 'Khara Beech' means: Shit In You (Female)

In Arabic, 'Nikomak' means: Fuck Your Mother

In Spanish, 'Pinche Cabron' means: Go And Get Fucked

In German, 'Fick Mich' means: Fuck Me

In Spanish, 'Desgraciado' means: Clown

In French, 'Va T'Faire Mètt, Connard' means: Fuck You, Asshole

In Chinese, 'D'lu Ne Lo Mo' means: Fuck Your Mom

In French, 'Les Fleurs' means: Fuck Off

In Chinese (Fu Tso Hua), 'Sa Nù Ne, Nù Ne Wòi Sa' means: Fuck Your Mother

In Spanish, 'Puta' means: Tu Suck

In French, 'Un Trou Du Cul' means: Asshole

In French, 'De La Merde' means: Its Just A Bunch Of Shit(Lit)

In French, 'Bouffon' means: Asshole

In Italian, 'Pezzo Di Merda   ' means: Piece Of Shit

In Chinese (Hokkien), " means: Fuck Your Bloody Mother'S Pussy

In Spanish, 'Chupame La Polla' means: To Shit

In Japanese, 'Oni' means: Demon

In Chinese (Mandarin), 'Chao Ni Niang' means: Fuck Your Mom

In Japanese, " means: I Enjoy Pussy Very Much

In Spanish, 'Panocha' means: Little Dick

In German, 'Blödes Arschloch' means: Stupid Asshole

In Japanese, 'Ookiosewada' means: Up Yours

In Arabic, 'Zarba' means: Shit

In Arabic, 'Koos' means: Cunt.

In Italian, 'No Skuche Ala Gats! ' means: What The Fuck Do You

In Chinese, 'Gai' means: Whore

In Arabic, 'Muti' means: Jackass

In Chinese (Hokkien), 'Peh Bu Ki Ho Gao Kan' means: Parents Go Fuck By Dogs

In French, 'Cul' means: Ass

In Chinese (Hokkien), 'Neh' means: Breast

In Chinese, 'Tiu Nia Ma Chow Hai' means: Fuck Your Mom'S Smelly Cunt

In Spanish, 'Chinga Tu Madre' means: Breasts

In Japanese, 'Pai Pai' means: Breasts, Nipples

In Chinese, 'Sek Si' means: Eat Shit

In Hindi, 'Chut Choot' means: Pussy

In French, 'Nique Ta Mère' means: Fuck Your Mom

In Arabic, 'Waj Ab Zibik!' means: An Infection To Your Dick

In Japanese, 'Achike' means: Fuck Off

In Chinese, 'Poq Gai' means: Go Die In The Street

In French, 'Ta Mère Est Une Salope' means: Your Mother Is A Bitch

In Italian, 'Merda ' means: Shit

In Chinese, 'Chow Fah Hai' means: Smelly Cheap Cunt

In Japanese, 'Oh Baka' means: Biggest Idiot

In German, 'Dummes Huhn' means: Stupid Chicken

In Hindi, 'Gaand Gaa' means: Nd

In French, 'Bite' means: Cock

In French, 'Un Con, Une Conasse' means: Moron, Asshole

In German, 'Arschgesicht' means: Butthead

In French, 'Pauv' Conne' means: Stupid Bitch

In Italian, 'Vaffanculo ' means: Go Fuck Yourself

In French, 'Va Te Branler ' means: Go Play With Yourself

In Hindi, 'Tatti' means: Shit

In Chinese, 'Lok Chat' means: Dick

In Arabic, 'Elif Air Ab Dinich' means: A Thousand Dicks In Your Religion

In Japanese, 'Baka' means: Idiot

In Spanish, 'Metete Un Palo Por El Culo' means: Son Of Thousand Bitches

In German, 'Dummkopf' means: Stupid

In Chinese (Hokkien), 'Sai Ne Niang' means: Shit On Your Mother

In Arabic, 'Maaras' means: Pimp

In Italian, 'Cazzo Vai Via Stronzo ' means: Shit, Get Out Of Here Jerk

In Arabic, 'Kanith' means: Fucker

In Japanese, 'Baka Yaro ' means: Stupid Bastard

In Japanese, 'Urusai, Kono Bakayaro' means: Shut Up You Noisy Idiot

In Chinese (Hokkien), 'Lan Hoot' means: Balls

In Chinese (Hokkien), " means: Fuck Your Fore

In Italian, 'Puttana ' means: Whore

In Hindi, 'Jhaant Ke Bal' means: Pubic Hair

In French, 'Vas Te Faire Foutre' means: Go Get Fucked

In Spanish, 'Chichi' means: Cunt

In Japanese, 'Baka Kuso Atama' means: Stupid Shit Head

In French, 'Va Te Tripoter' means: Go Tinker With Yourself

In Chinese (Hokkien), 'Keh' means: Whore

In Chinese (Hokkien), 'Ni Na Bu' means: Your Fucking Mother

In Japanese, 'Kisama' means: Lord Of The Donkeys

In Japanese, 'Onara' means: Fart

In Chinese (Hakka), 'Guy' means: Whore

In Spanish, 'Calientapollas' means: Unlucky, Son Of A Bitch

In Spanish, 'Pendeja' means: Fuck Your Mom

In Japanese, 'Minikui' means: Ugly

In French, 'Chienne, Salope, Putain' means: Bitch

In German, 'Verpiss Dich' means: Piss Off

In German, 'Schlampe' means: Tramp Or Slut

In Hindi, ' Maa' means: Duhr Chod

In German, 'Fotze' means: Cunt

In Chinese (Hakka), 'Diao Nia Meh' means: Fuck Your Mom

In German, 'Scheisskopf ' means: Shithead

In Chinese, 'Fei Hai' means: Fat Cunt

In Spanish, 'Cabron' means: Fuck Off You

In French, 'Vas Te Branler ' means: Fuck Yourself

In Spanish, 'Me Cago En La Leche!' means: Fucking Damn It

BONUS!!!

Link to download free printable PDF habit tracker.

https://rwsquaredmedia.wordpress.com/free-habit-tracker/

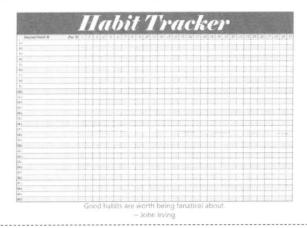

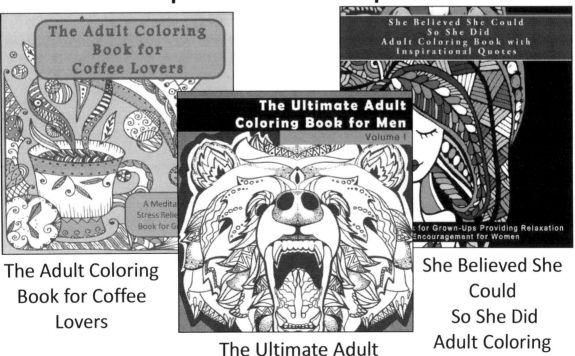

The Adult Coloring
Book for Coffee
Lovers

The Ultimate Adult
Coloring Book for Men

She Believed She
Could
So She Did
Adult Coloring
Book

Made in the USA
Columbia, SC
19 December 2017